Instant Pot Cookbook for Beginners

Simple and Easy Everyday Recipes for Instant Pot Newbies

Julie Bower

Table of Contents

Introduction 6
Chapter 1: What is Instant Pot? 7
Chapter 2: How to use Instant Pot 9
Chapter 3: Benefits of using Instant Pot 12
Chapter 4: Instant Pot Recipes 14
Breakfast Recipes: 14
   Creamy Polenta 14
   Spiced Apple Oatmeal 16
   Bacon and Cheese Crustless Quiche 18
   Steel-Cut Breakfast Oats 20
   Coconut Cornmeal Porridge 22
   Cranberry Apricot Steel-Cut Oats 24
   Black Bean and Egg Casserole 26
   Sausage & Scrambled Eggs 28
Soups & Stews, Chili 30
   Turmeric Chicken Soup 30
   Salmon Stew 32
   Cream of Broccoli Soup 34
   Swiss Chard Stem Soup 36
   Butternut and Cauliflower Stew 38
   Red Lentil Chili 40
   Instant Pot Ham and Potato Soup 42
   Classic Beef Chili 44
   White Chicken Chili 46
   Beans and Tomato Stew 48
Main 50

Beef & Pork & Lamb 50

- Mexican Pulled Pork 50
- Instant Pot Pork Ribs 52
- Balsamic Pot Roast 54
- BBQ Beef Ribs 56
- Beef Vegetable Stew 58
- Beef and Broccoli Stir Fry 60
- Coffee Pork Ribs 62
- Maple Spice Rubbed Ribs 64
- BBQ Pulled Pork 66
- Orange-Glazed Pork Chops 67
- Lamb Stew 70
- Garlic Pork Tenderloin 72
- Instant Pot Lamb Shanks 73
- Lamb Rogan Josh 75
- Marinara Beef Meatballs 78
- Mushroom Beef Stroganoff 80
- Instant Pot Lamb Chops 82
- Pork Sausages and Mushrooms 84

Poultry 86

- Lemongrass and Coconut Chicken 86
- Honey Sesame Chicken 88
- Instant Pot Cashew Chicken 90
- Instant Pot Shredded Chicken 92
- Instant Pot Chicken Cacciatore 93
- Honey Teriyaki Chicken 96
- Instant Pot BBQ Chicken with Potatoes 98
- Chicken with White Wine Mushroom Sauce 99

- Root Beer Chicken Wings 102
- Sticky Chicken and Chilies 103
- Balsamic Orange Chicken Drumsticks 106
- Ginger Turkey and Potatoes 108
- Turkey and Pomegranate Mix 110
- Chicken Wings and Scallions Sauce 112
- Turkey and Cauliflower Sauté 114
- Turkey and Mushrooms Meatballs 116
- Lime Turkey Wings 118

Seafood 120
- Spicy Prawns 120
- Thai Fish Curry 122
- Buttered Trout 123
- Spicy Chili Garlic Trout 124
- Spicy Lemon Halibut 125
- Green Chili Mahi Mahi 126
- Wild Alaskan Cod.. 128
- Instant Pot Shrimps 129
- Crabs in Coconut Milk 130
- Instant Pot Seafood Stew 131
- Lobster with Wine and Tomatoes 134
- Creamy Haddock with Kale 136

Vegetable mains 138
- Curried Squash Stew 138
- Instant Pot Zucchini Casserole 140
- Creamy Artichoke, Garlic, and Zucchini 142
- Rosemary Garlic Potatoes 144
- Sweet Sticky Carrots 146

- Instant Pot Steamed Artichoke 148
- Simple Green Beans Salad 150
- Simple Eggplant Spread 152
- Instant Pot Mashed Potatoes 154

Desserts 156
- Sweet Apple Pudding 156
- Pumpkin and Rice Pudding 158
- Steamed Carrot Cake 160
- Instant Pot Cherry Compote 162
- Instant Pot Raspberry Curd 164
- Apple Cinnamon Cake 166
- Cranberry Stuffed Apples 168

Conclusion 170

Introduction

The Instant Pot is a versatile kitchen device that acts as a multi-cooker. It can function as a slow cooker, pressure cooker, rice cooker, steamer, warmer, and more. You can use it to sear, brown and sauté food, as well as bake breads and pastries. It can even be used to make yogurt. That's how versatile and convenient this kitchen tool is.

One of the biggest highlights of owning an instant pot is its ability to save cooking time in the kitchen. Many of us have similar goals of wanting to eat healthier, but we don't have hours to spend prepping healthy ingredients. This is where the instant pot becomes a true lifesaver! Meals that typically take 4-6 hours to cook can literally be cooked in as little as 30-40 minutes! All you need to do is to drop all ingredients in the pot, select the right cooking setting, and wait for your meal to cook. Enjoy the best of instant pot meals found in this book with ready to get ingredients and simple instructions for a beginner.

Chapter 1: What is Instant Pot?

It is a multifunctional kitchen appliance that cooks fast, saving you time while at the same time retaining the nutritional values of your ingredients. It is automated and easy to use. It works as a warming pot, rice cooker, slow cooker, and an electric pressure cooker.

The basic Instant Pot comes with the unit itself, a lid, an interior pot, a plastic piece to collect condensation, a trivet and utensils. Assembling the unit is very intuitive, you plug in the power cord, place the interior pot into the Instant Pot, place the lid on top, and you are good to go. You will find the spot for the condensation collector to slide into place on the back of the Instant Pot, near the base. In general, you will not see much condensation collect back here; it is only for heavy flow scenarios.

The lid of the Instant Pot warrants a closer look as you will frequently be dealing with the steamer function which will, in turn, require caution as the steam will easily be hot enough to cause burns that may not be serious, but will certainly be painful. To lock the lid, you are going to move the steam release handle into the sealing position. The top of the lid also features a float valve that pushes up from inside of the lid. This valve will be down when the Instant Pot is not at a maximum pressure which serves as a visual indicator as to if it is safe to open or not.

Inside of the lid you will see where the float valve connects, along with the exhaust valve which is covered to keep it working properly. You will want to practice removing the covering of the exhaust valve before you use the Instant Pot to ensure you know what you are doing before it needs cleaning. Regular cleaning of the exhaust valve is key to ensuring your Instant Pot remains at peak functionality. Occasionally, you will also need to clean the float valve, to do so you will need to remove the silicone covering beforehand, it should come off easily as long as it is cleaned regularly.

The sealing ring which sits on a metal rack in the inside of the lid can also be removed for cleaning purposes. It is important to be extremely careful with this sealing ring as if it is stretched in any way, it will be impossible for the Instant Pot to generate a reliable seal, severely limiting its versatility. The lid can also be propped open by simply inserting one of the fins into the notch in the handle on the base of the Instant Pot.

To close the Instant Pot securely, all you need to do is to place the lid on the unit so the arrows on the cooker and the arrows on the lid line up. Turning the lid will then align the arrow on the lid to align with the closed lock picture on the base. This will require a clockwise movement and will be accompanied by a chime if the unit is plugged in. Opening the Instant Pot requires a counter-clockwise movement and will also be accompanied by a chime if the unit is plugged in.

Chapter 2: How to use Instant Pot

When cooking food using an Instant pot, you will come across the following functions:

Keep Warm/Cancel Button

This button is pretty self-explanatory. You press this button to either cancel a cooking function or if you want to switch off your Instant Pot.

Sauté Button

This function is to sauté your ingredients in the pot, just as how you sauté things in a pot.

Manual Button

This button has an all-purpose function. If your recipe mentions cooking on high-pressure for a specific cook time- use this button. You can adjust the cooking time with the '+' or '-indicators. There are also pre-set buttons that you can use instead of the manual one. Most pressure cooking recipes already come with instructions on how many hours and minutes you need to cook a meal for. But with the Instant Cooker Pot, it makes your life easier if in the event you do not have any available recipes or if you want to build or make something from scratch. The preset buttons guide you into determining the amount of time needed for an individual meal.

Here's a list of these buttons and what they can do for pressure cooking:

To make soup

For delicious soups, pressure-cook them on high for 30 minutes cook time. Simply put all your ingredients in the pot, press the 'Soup' time and the 'Adjust' button once (more) increase cook time to forty minutes. If you want to cook for twenty minutes, press 'Soup' and 'Adjust' twice (less) to cook for less time. No more slaving over the stove to make the perfect soup.

For meat & stews

High-pressure cook time is required for 35 minutes for meats and stews, so the meat drops off the bone. To adjust more, click on Adjust more to cook for 45 minutes and to cook less, adjust less to cook for 20 minutes.

For Beans & Chili

30-minute cook time on high-pressure is required. To add more time, press 'Adjust' '+' to increase to 45 minutes and '-'to decrease to 25 minutes.

For Poultry

You want the meat tender but not too flaky, so the cook time for this is 15 minutes of high pressure. Of course, you can adjust to a 30-minute cook time with '+' or 25-minute cook time with '-.'

For Rice

Rice needs to be fluffy. Too much water and it's lumpy and too little water will make your rice undercooked and dry. The rice function is the only fully automatic programming on the Instant Pot Cooker. The electronic programming adjusts cooking time depending on the ratio of water and rice that you put in the cooking pot.

For Multi-Grain

Ideal to be cooked on high pressure for 40 minutes cook time. If you need to soak them, and then adjust the timer to 45 minutes soaking and 60 minutes cook time.

For Porridge and Congee

The texture you are looking for is soft and somewhat lumpy. Cook on high pressure for 20 minutes. To add more time, press Adjust '+' to cook for 30 minutes. For less adjust '-for 15 min cook time.

For Steaming

Use a steamer basket or a rack for this function because you want to prevent the food from having to touch the bottom of the pot when it heats at full power. You can cook on high pressure for just 10 minutes. Once the pot reaches the desired pressure, the steam button automatically regulates pressure. Use the '+' or '-buttons to adjust cook time or use the Pressure button to change the fixed timing for lower or higher temperature.

Chapter 3: Benefits of using Instant Pot

Perfectly Cooked Meals

With the Instant Pot, you can make all types of perfectly cooked foods like pot roast in one pot. You can then "keep warm" using the 24-hour programmable timer. It spares you from using a skillet to brown your meat and sears in the juices. You won't need to be home to turn it to "keep warm" setting after the cooking process is over, as the device will do that by itself. You can come home to perfectly cooked pot roast that is tender and tasty without falling apart into smithereens.

No Mess, Easy Clean

You have almost no mess to clean and wash after you are done with cooking because you have only used one pot for everything, which gets clean in no time.

Instant Pot comes with a removable stainless-steel inner cooking basket. Simply remove it and place in the dishwasher or rinse with soapy water. A simple wipe-down with a cloth on the outside and that's it. It spares you from heavy cleaning of your pots and pans.

Multifunctional

It can be used as a warming pot, slow cooker, pressure cooker, and rice cooker. It is also used to bake and also make yogurt, making it an all-in-one appliance which saves you the need to buy other appliances.

Energy Efficient & Safe

Instant Pot is capable of cooking your foods fast using high-pressure steam and generating a high temperature; it can save up to 70% of electric consumption by taking less time to cook. It has been designed to concentrate energy only on cooking the added ingredients to prevent energy waste.

Space Saving

If you are always fighting for the space in your kitchen, then Instant Pot is for you. Since you can pressure cook, slow cook, sauté, and brown along with multiple cooking setting mentioned earlier, you don't need to purchase multiple utensils as owning Instant Pot only is just enough. Its compact design takes less space and you can easily store it in your kitchen cabinet or countertop.

Food retains more nutrients

When pressure cooking, heat is distributed more evenly, and less water is used in the processing, so nutrients are not lost. Not only does food retain its nutrients, but it also retains its color. Green beans stay green instead of turning gray. And the texture is much more appealing; not soggy, mushy vegetables!

Chapter 4: Instant Pot Recipes

Breakfast Recipes:

Creamy Polenta

Prep time: 5 minutes
Cook time: 20 minutes
Servings: 2

Nutritional Information:

- Calories: 139
- Fat: 0 g
- Carbs: 30 g

- Protein: 2 g

Ingredients:

- Polenta, ½ cup
- Water, 2 cups
- Salt, ¼ tsp.

Directions:

1. Put all the ingredients into the Instant pot and stir well
2. Switch the vent to sealed position with the lid locked
3. Select Porridge setting and cook for 20 minutes.
4. When the timer sounds, allow the pressure to release naturally.
5. Open the lid once pin in the lid drops.
6. Stir polenta with a wooden spoon.
7. Add your favorite toppings (butter, pepper, cheese)

Spiced Apple Oatmeal

Prep time:

5 minutes

Cooking time:

17 minutes

Servings: 2

Nutritional Information:

- Calories: 254
- Fat: 13 g
- Carbs: 33 g
- Protein: 3 g

Ingredients:

- Butter, 2 tbsp.
- Steel cut oats, ½ cup
- Boiling water, 1¼ cups
- Apple, ½
- Sugar, 2 tbsp.
- Ground cinnamon, ¼ tsp.
- Salt

Directions:

1. Select Sauté. Melt the butter in the Instant Pot.
2. Add the oats and stir for about 5 minutes until lightly toasted.
3. Stir in the remaining ingredients and make sure the oats are covered with water.
4. Secure the lid on. Cancel Sauté and select Pressure Cook for 12 minutes.
5. Release pressure naturally for 10 minutes.
6. Serve with a knob of butter, maple syrup and a splash of cream or milk if desired.

Bacon and Cheese Crustless Quiche

Prep time: 5 minutes

Cook time: 10 minutes

Servings: 3

Nutritional Information:

- Calories: 396
- Carbs: 5 g
- Fat: 31 g
- Protein: 23 g

Ingredients:

- Lightly beaten eggs, 6
- Milk, 1 cup
- Pepper
- Grayed Monterey Jack cheese, 2 cups
- Salt
- Cooked and crumbled bacon, 1 cup

Directions:

1. Use the cooking spray to spray the inner pot of the instant pot.

2. In a mixing bowl, add the eggs, milk, salt, and pepper then mix until well-combined.
3. Place the bacon and cheese in the Instant Pot and pour over the egg mixture.
4. Select the manual function with the lid closed then set the cook time to 10 minutes.
5. Do natural pressure release.

Steel-Cut Breakfast Oats

Prep time: 3 minutes

Cook time: 4 minutes

Servings: 2

Nutritional Information:
- Calories: 330
- Fat: 4 g
- Carbs: 83 g
- Protein: 10 g

Ingredients:
- Steel cut oats, 1 cup
- Plain Greek yogurt, 1 cup

- Water, 1 ½ cups
- Chopped apples, 2
- Maple syrup, ¼ cup
- Cloves, ½ tsp.
- Cinnamon powder, ½ tsp.
- Slivered almonds, 2 tbsp.

Directions:

1. Place the oats in the Instant Pot.
2. Stir in the water, yogurt, apples, maple syrup, cloves, and cinnamon.
3. Close the lid and seal the valve.
4. Press the Manual button and cook for 4 minutes.
5. Do quick pressure release.
6. Stir again and garnish with slivered almonds and more maple syrup or cinnamon.

Coconut Cornmeal Porridge

Prep time: 15 minutes
Cook time: 6 minutes
Servings: 6

Nutritional Information:

- Calories: 253
- Fat: 3 g
- Carbs: 46 g
- Protein: 6 g

Ingredients:

- Water, 6 cups
- Coconut milk, 1¼ cups
- Yellow cornmeal, 1¼ cups
- Cinnamon sticks, 2½
- Vanilla extract, 1¼ tsp.
- Coconut flakes, ¾ tsp.
- Sweetened condensed milk, ¾ cup

Directions:

1. Pour 5 cups of water and all the coconut milk to the Instant Pot.

2. Mix the cornmeal with 1 cup of water then add the mixture to the pot.
3. Add vanilla extract, coconut flakes, and cinnamon sticks.
4. Select the manual function with the lid closed then set the cook time to 6 minutes at high pressure.
5. Release the pressure naturally once the timer clicks.
6. Remove the lid then add the sweetened condensed milk and stir.
7. Serve and enjoy.

Cranberry Apricot Steel-Cut Oats

/**Prep time:** 5 minutes
Cook time: 10 minutes
Serves: 4

Nutritional Information:

- Calories: 351
- Fat: 16 g
- Carbs: 45 g
- Protein: 6 g

Ingredients:

- Steel-cut oats, 2 cups
- Water, 3 cups
- Butter, 4 tbsp.
- Squeezed orange juice, 2 cups
- Dried cranberries, 2 tbsp.
- Raisins, 2 tbsp.
- Chopped dried apricots, 2 tbsp.
- Maple syrup, 2 tbsp.
- Ground cinnamon, ½ tsp.

- Chopped pecans, 4 tbsp.
- Salt, ¼ tsp.
- Chopped Strawberries

Directions:

1. Put all ingredients into the Instant Pot.
2. Select the manual function with the lid closed then set the cook time to 10 minutes at high pressure
3. Release the pressure naturally once the timer is over and remove the lid
4. Stir the meal gently the serve topped with strawberries.

Black Bean and Egg Casserole

Prep time: 10 minutes
Cook time: 23 minutes
Servings: 3.

Nutritional Information:
- Calories: 564
- Fat: 30 g
- Carbs: 33 g
- Protein: 36 g

Ingredients:
- Large beaten eggs, 4
- Ground sausage, ½ lb.
- Chopped red onion, ¼

- Chopped red bell pepper, ½
- Pre-cooked black beans, ½ lb.
- Green onions, ¼ cup
- Wheat flour, ¼ cup
- Cotija cheese, ½ cup
- Mozzarella cheese, ½ cup

Directions:

1. Put the sausage and onion to the Instant Pot and select the "Sauté" function and cook for 3 minutes.
2. Mix the flour with eggs and add this mixture to the sausages.
3. Add all the vegetables, cheeses, and beans.
4. Select the manual function with the lid sealed then adjust the cook time to 20 minutes at high pressure
5. Release the pressure naturally once the timer clicks and remove the lid
6. Remove the inner pot, place a plate on top then flip the pot to transfer the casserole to the plate.
7. Serve warm.

Sausage & Scrambled Eggs

/Prep time: 2 minutes
Cook time: 5 minutes
Servings: 2

Nutritional Information:

- Calories: 212
- Fat: 17 g
- Carbs: 2 g
- Protein: 11 g

Ingredients:

- Oil, 1 tbsp.
- Pork sausage, 1
- Eggs, 3
- Milk, ¼ cup
- Salt
- Pepper

Directions:

1. Select Sauté. Add oil to the Instant Pot and heat.

2. Add the sausage and fry well. Once cooked, remove and slice as thinly as desired.
3. In a mixing bowl, whisk together the rest of the ingredients and set aside.
4. Return the sausage to the Instant Pot and select Sauté.
5. Add the set aside mixture and gently push the mixture around until cooked to desired doneness.
6. Serve with toast or freshly sliced tomato.

Soups & Stews, Chili

Turmeric Chicken Soup

Prep time: 5 minutes
Cook time: 15 minutes
Servings: 4

Nutritional information:

- Calories: 599
- Carbs: 3 g
- Protein: 46 g
- Fat: 61 g

Ingredients:

- Coconut milk, ½ cup
- Turmeric powder, 2½ tsp.
- Water, 4 cups
- Bay leaf, 1
- De-boned chicken breasts, 3

Directions:

- In the Instant Pot, put all ingredients and stir well.
- Switch the vent points to "Sealing." Then close the lid.
- Select the poultry function and 15 minutes cook time
- Release the pressure naturally when the timer clicks.

Salmon Stew

Prep time: 5 minutes
Cook time: 16 minutes
Servings: 3

Nutritional Information:

- Calories: 825
- Carbs: 2 g
- Protein: 46 g
- Fat: 94 g

Ingredients:

- Minced garlic cloves, 3
- Salmon fillets, 8 oz.

- Pepper, ¼ tsp.
- Olive oil, 3 tbsp.
- Salt, ¼ tsp.
- Water, 3 cups
- Spinach, 1 bunch

Directions:

1. Click on the Sauté function on the Instant Pot and heat the olive oil.
2. Fry the garlic for 3 minutes.
3. Add water, pepper, salmon fillets, and salt.
4. Switch the vent to sealing with the lid closed
5. Select manual button and set the cook time to 10 minutes
6. Release the pressure naturally once the timer clicks.
7. Open the lid and select the Sauté function then add the spinach.
8. Allow to simmer for 3 minutes.

Cream of Broccoli Soup

Prep time: 5 minutes

Cook time: 34 minutes

Servings: 4

Nutritional Information:
- Calories: 118
- Carbs: 2 g
- Protein: 7 g
- Fat: 10 g

Ingredients:
- Paprika powder, 1 tsp.
- Chicken bones, ½ lb.

- Sliced broccoli heads, 2
- Water, 4 cups
- Sliced small avocado, 1

Directions:

1. Put the chicken bones and water in the Instant Pot.
2. Add pepper and salt
3. Switch the vent to sealing then close the lid
4. Select the manual button and set cooking time to 30 minutes
5. Do quick pressure release when the time is over
6. Remove the lid and discard the bones.
7. Add the broccoli and stir well
8. Select manual button with the lid sealed then cook for 4 minutes
9. Do quick pressure release.
10. Transfer everything into a blender. Add the avocado slices.
11. Mix until smooth.
12. Place in a bowl and sprinkle with paprika powder.

Swiss Chard Stem Soup

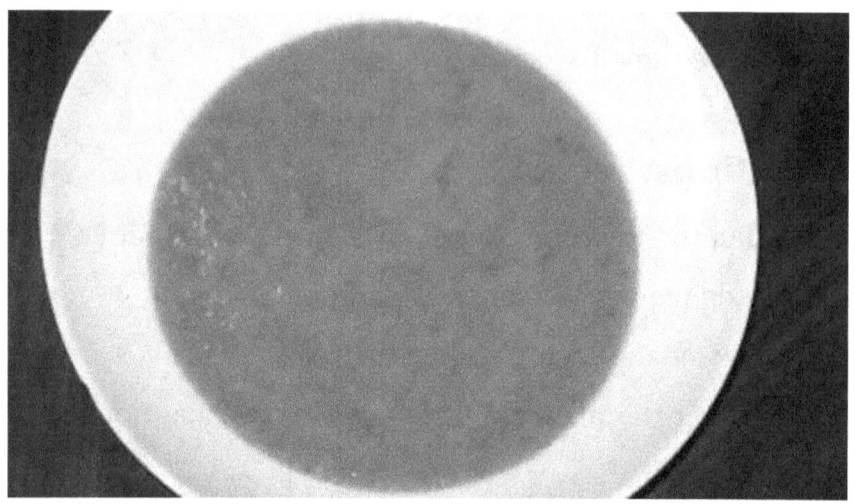

Prep time: 3 minutes
Cook time: 4 minutes
Servings: 4

Nutritional Information:

- Calories: 200
- Carbs: 24 g
- Protein: 5 g
- Fat: 11 g

Ingredients:

- Diced potato, 1
- Chopped leeks, 3

- Pepper.
- Diced celeriac, 1
- Coconut milk, 1 cup
- Salt
- Chicken stock, 1½ cups
- Diced Swiss Chard stems, 8 cups

Directions:

1. In the instant pot, put all the ingredients and stir well
2. Select the manual button and close the lid.
3. Cook for 4 minutes.
4. Release the pressure naturally when the timer clicks.

Butternut and Cauliflower Stew

Prep time: 5 minutes

Cook time: 12 minutes

Servings: 3

Nutritional Information:

- Calories: 244
- Carbs: 18 g
- Protein: 3 g
- Fat: 2 g

Ingredients:

- Red pepper flakes, ½ tsp.
- Sliced cauliflower head, 1
- Olive oil, 1 tsp.
- Paprika, 1 tsp.
- 3 minced garlic cloves
- Chopped butternut squash, 1 lb.
- Chopped onion, 1

- Dried thyme, 1 tsp.
- Salt
- Vegetable broth, 2 cups
- Whole milk, ½ cup

Directions:

1. Select the Sauté button on the Instant Pot.
2. Pour in the oil and sauté the onion and garlic until fragrant.
3. Add the rest of the ingredients.
4. Close the lid and press the Soup button.
5. Adjust the cooking time to 12 minutes.
6. Release the pressure naturally when the timer clicks.
7. Serve topped with chopped parsley

Red Lentil Chili

Prep time: 5 minutes
Cook time: 60 minutes
Servings: 7

Nutritional Information:

- Calories: 188
- Carbs: 34 g
- Protein: 12 g
- Fat: 1 g

Ingredients:

- Salt

- Water, 7 cups
- Apple cider vinegar, 4 tbsp.
- Crushed tomatoes, 2 cans
- Chopped Medjool dates, ¼ cup
- Oregano, 1½ tbsp.
- Tomato paste, 2 tbsp.
- Chopped red bell peppers, 2 cups
- Minced garlic cloves, 8
- Pepper.
- Soaked and rinsed red lentils, 1 lb.
- Flaked parsley, 1 ½ tbsp.
- Chili powder, 1 ½ tbsp.

Directions:

1. In the Instant Pot, put all the ingredients and stir well.
2. Select the manual button with the lid closed
3. Adjust the cooking time to 60 minutes.
4. Release the pressure naturally once cooked

Instant Pot Ham and Potato Soup

Prep time: 5 minutes

Cook time: 28 minutes

Servings: 4

Nutritional Information:
- Calories: 394
- Carbs: 47 g
- Protein: 25 g
- Fat: 13 g

Ingredients:
- Cayenne pepper
- Butter, 2 tbsp.

- Diced onion, 1
- Diced cooked ham, 1 cup
- Sliced potatoes, 2 lbs.
- Pepper.
- Chicken broth, 4 cups
- Grated cheddar cheese, ½ cup
- Fried bacon bits, 2 tbsp.
- Salt
- 8 minced garlic cloves

Directions:

1. Select the Sauté button on the Instant Pot.
2. Heat the butter and sauté the onions and garlic until fragrant then add the potatoes.
3. Cook for 3 minutes as you stir then add the broth, pepper, cheese, cayenne pepper, salt, and cooked ham.
4. Press the Manual button with the lid closed.
5. Set the cooking time to 25 minutes.
6. Release the pressure naturally once cooked.
7. Remove the lid and serve immediately.

Classic Beef Chili

Prep time: 5 minutes
Cook time: 20 minutes
Servings: 4

Nutritional Information:

- Calories: 249
- Carbs: 22 g
- Protein: 27 g
- Fat: 6 g

Ingredients:
- Diced onion, 1
- Chili powder, 1 tbsp.
- Diced bell pepper, 1

- Ground beef, 2 lb.
- Minced garlic cloves, 3
- Green chilies, 1 cup
- Cumin, 2/3 tbsp.
- Ketchup, ¼ cup
- Salt, Pepper
- Ground cumin, 1 tsp.
- Brown sugar, ½ tbsp.
- Red wine, 1/3 cup
- Hot sauce, 1 tsp.
- Diced tomatoes, 1 can
- Chicken broth, 2 cups
- Kidney beans, 2 cans rinsed and drained

Directions:

1. Select the Sauté function and add the beef, garlic, and onions.
2. Cook for 3 minutes as you stir
3. Add the remaining ingredients and stir well.
4. Select the manual function with the lid sealed
5. Set the cooking time to 15 minutes.
6. Release the pressure naturally once the timer is over
7. Serve with cilantro or avocado slices

White Chicken Chili

Prep time: 5 minutes
Cook time: 20 minutes
Servings: 4

Nutritional Information:

- Calories: 608
- Carbs: 38 g
- Protein: 41 g
- Fat: 32 g

Ingredients:

- Cream of chicken soup, 1 can
- Oil, 2 tbsp.
- Diced onion, 1
- Chicken broth, 1 cup
- Taco seasoning, 1 packet
- Northern beans, 2 cans
- Chicken thighs, 2 lbs.
- Pepper.
- Corn kernels, 1 cup
- Minced garlic cloves, 3

- Chopped green chilies, 1 cup
- Salt
- Grated Monterey Jack cheese, 1 cup

Directions:
1. Select the Sauté button on the Instant Pot.
2. Put in the chicken thighs, onions, and garlic until fragrant.
3. Add the remaining ingredients.
4. Select the manual function with the lid closed.
5. Set the cooking time to 15 minutes.
6. Release the pressure naturally once the timer clicks.

Beans and Tomato Stew

Prep time: 5 minutes

Cook time: 60 minutes

Servings: 4

Nutritional Information:

- Calories: 312
- Carbs: 49 g
- Protein: 16 g
- Fat: 7 g

Ingredients:

- Ground cinnamon, 1 ½ tsp.
- Mild paprika, 1 ½ tbsp.
- Olive oil, 2 tbsp.
- Vegetable broth, 3 cup.
- Soaked and drained chickpeas, 1 cup
- 1 chopped onion
- Chopped celery stalks, 2
- Pepper.
- Dried dill, 1½ tsp.
- Diced tomatoes, 1 cup

- Salt
- Soaked and drained white beans, 1 cup
- Tomato paste, 2 tbsp.

Directions:

1. In the Instant Pot, put all the ingredients and stir well.
2. Select the manual function with the lid closed.
3. Adjust the cooking time to 30 minutes.
4. Release the pressure quickly once the timer clicks

Main
Beef & Pork & Lamb
Mexican Pulled Pork

Prep time: 5 minutes
Cook time: 1 hour 30 minutes
Servings: 5

Nutritional Information:
- Calories: 364
- Carbs: 1 g
- Protein: 20 g
- Fat: 36 g

Ingredients:

- Cinnamon, 1 tsp.
- Coconut oil, 5 tbsp.
- Cumin powder, 1 tsp.
- Pork shoulder, 4 lb.
- Garlic powder, 2 tsp.

Directions:

1. Into the Instant Pot, add all the ingredients and pour 1½ cups of water.
2. Season with salt and pepper to taste.
3. Switch the vent to sealing and close the lid
4. Select the Meat/Stew button and adjust the time to 1 hour and 30 minutes.
5. Release the pressure naturally once the timer clicks
6. Once the lid is open, take the meat out and shred using two forks.

Instant Pot Pork Ribs

Prep time: 5 minutes
Cook time: 8 hours
Servings: 3

Nutritional Information:
- Calories: 1375
- Carbs: 6 g
- Protein: 98 g
- Fat: 105 g

Ingredients:
- Garlic powder, 1 tbsp.
- Olive oil, 5 tbsp.
- Rack baby back ribs, 1
- Smoked paprika, 1 tbsp.
- Onion powder, 1 tbsp.
- Pepper
- Salt

Directions:

1. Put the baby back ribs on a baking sheet and season with the rest of the ingredients until they coat well.
2. Transfer the ribs into the instant pot and add ½ cup water
3. Switch the vent to venting with the lid closed
4. Select the Slow Cook function and adjust the time to 8 hours.

Balsamic Pot Roast

Prep time: 5 minutes
Cook time: 1 hour 15 minutes
Servings: 8

Nutritional Information:

- Calories: 398
- Carbs: 14 g
- Protein: 36 g
- Fat: 21 g

Ingredients:

- Bouillon powder, 1 tsp.
- Balsamic vinegar, ¼ cup

- Chuck roast, 4 lbs.
- Chopped onions, 2
- Scrubbed baby potatoes, 1 lb.
- Pepper.
- Olive oil, 1 tbsp.
- Minced garlic cloves, 8
- Chopped celery stalks, 2
- Salt
- Dijon mustard, 2 tbsp.
- Beef broth, 1 cup
- Brown sugar, 1 tbsp.
- Chopped carrots, 4

Directions:

1. Rub the pot roast with seasonings.
2. Select the Sauté function then heat the oil.
3. Add the pot roast and sear all sides, for 10 minutes.
4. Add the onions and garlic to cook for 5 minutes.
5. Add the remaining ingredients.
6. Select meat/stew button with the lid closed
7. Adjust the cooking time to 60 minutes.
8. Release the pressure naturally when the timer is over

BBQ Beef Ribs

Prep time: 5 minutes
Cook time: 60 minutes
Servings: 4

Nutritional Information:

- Calories: 689
- Carbs: 10 g
- Protein: 32 g
- Fat: 58 g

Ingredients:

- BBQ sauce, 2 cups
- Beef ribs, 3 lbs.
- Salt
- Beef broth, ½ cup
- Pepper.
- Pepper jelly, 2 tbsp.

Directions:

1. Rub the ribs with salt and pepper then transfer them into the instant pot
2. Add the remaining ingredients.

3. Select the meat/stew button with the lid closed
4. Adjust the cooking time to 40 minutes.
5. Release the pressure naturally once cooked.

Beef Vegetable Stew

Prep time: 4 minutes

Cook time: 35 minutes

Servings: 4

Nutritional Information:

- Calories: 295
- Carbs: 35 g
- Protein: 5 g
- Fat: 16 g

Ingredients:

- Worcestershire sauce, 2 tbsp.
- Green peas, 1 cup
- Sliced carrots, 2
- Garlic cloves, 2
- Tomato sauce, ½ cup
- Sliced beef stew meat, 2 lb.
- Pepper. Salt.
- Diced potatoes, 3
- Corn kernels, 1 cup
- Oil, 2 tbsp.

- Bay leaf, 1
- Vegetable broth, 2 cups
- Diced onion, 1

Directions:

1. Click on the Sauté function of the Instant Pot to heat the oil.
2. Sauté the onion and garlic for 2 minutes.
3. Add the beef and stir for another 3 minutes until lightly brown.
4. Select meat/stew function and set 30 minutes cooking time with the lid closed
5. Release the pressure naturally when the timer clicks.

Beef and Broccoli Stir Fry

Prep time: 5 minutes
Cook time: 30 minutes
Servings: 4

Nutritional Information:

- Calories: 500
- Carbs: 55 g
- Protein: 37 g
- Fat: 15 g

Ingredients:

- Broccoli florets, 1 head
- Olive oil, 1 tbsp.
- Soy sauce, 2 tbsp.
- Thinly sliced flank steak, 1 lb.
- Brown sugar, ¼ tsp.
- Grated ginger, 1 tbsp.
- Five spice powder, 1/3 tsp.
- Chopped onion, 1
- Water, 2 tbsp.
- Oyster sauce, ½ tbsp.
- Beef broth, 2 cups

- Minced garlic cloves, 3
- Cornstarch, 1 tbsp.

Directions:

1. Select the Sauté button on the Instant Pot.
2. Heat the oil and sauté the onions and garlic for 2 minutes.
3. Add the beef and stir for another 3 minutes until lightly brown.
4. Add the remaining ingredients except for the broccoli and cornstarch slurry.
5. Select the meat/stew function with the lid closed
6. Set the cooking time to 20 minutes.
7. Release the pressure naturally when the timer clicks.
8. Open the lid and select sauté function then add the cornstarch slurry and broccoli.
9. Leave to simmer until the sauce thickens, for about 5 minutes

Coffee Pork Ribs

Prep time: 3 minutes

Cook time: 40 minutes

Servings: 3

Nutritional Information:
- Calories: 898
- Carbs: 4 g
- Protein: 77 g
- Fat: 64 g

Ingredients:
- Oyster sauce, 3 tbsp.
- Baby back ribs, 1 rack

- Liquid smoke, ½ cup
- Salt, 1 tsp.
- Instant coffee powder, 2 tbsp.
- Sugar, 1 tsp.
- Water, 1 cup
- Sesame oil, 2 tsp.

Directions:

1. Put all ingredients in the Instant Pot.
2. Select meat/stew function with the lid closed
3. Set the cooking time to 40 minutes.
4. Release the pressure naturally when the timer is over

Maple Spice Rubbed Ribs

Prep time: 4 minutes
Cook time: 45 minutes
Servings: 4

Nutritional Information:

- Calories: 955
- Carbs: 19 g
- Protein: 79 g
- Fat: 64 g

Ingredients:

- Ground ginger, ¼ tsp.

- Maple syrup, 4 tbsp.
- Salt
- Chili powder, 3 tbsp.
- Garlic powder, 1¼ tsp.
- Ground cinnamon, ¼ tsp.
- Ground coriander, 1¼ tsp.
- Pepper.
- Baby back ribs, 3½ lbs.
- Tomato sauce, 1 cup

Directions:

1. Into the Instant Pot, put all the ingredients and close the lid
2. Select the meat/stew function the set cook time to 35 minutes.
3. Release the pressure naturally once the timer is over.

BBQ Pulled Pork

Prep time: 5 minutes
Cook time: 60 minutes
Servings: 3

Nutritional Information:

- Calories: 318
- Carbs: 2 g
- Protein: 43 g
- Fat: 15 g

Ingredients:

- Chicken broth, ½ cup
- Pepper.
- BBQ sauce, ½ cup
- Salt
- Pork roast, 3 lbs.

Directions:

1. Put all ingredients in the Instant Pot then close the lid.
2. Select the meat/stew function and set the cook time to 60 minutes.
3. Release the pressure naturally.
4. Open the lid then shred the meat with two forks then serve with a sauce.

Orange-Glazed Pork Chops

Prep time: 5 minutes
Cook time: 30 minutes
Servings: 4

Nutritional Information:

- Calories: 582
- Carbs: 31 g
- Protein: 55 g
- Fat: 27 g

Ingredients:

- Orange marmalade, ½ cup
- Olive oil, 1 tbsp.
- Pork chops, 4
- Salt
- Onion powder, ¼ tsp.
- Chicken broth, 1 cup
- Pepper.
- Apple cider vinegar, 1 tbsp.
- Dried thyme, ¼ tsp.
- Orange zest, 1 tsp.

- Soy sauce, 2 tbsp.

Directions:
1. Sprinkle some seasonings on the pork chops
2. Press the Sauté function on the Instant Pot then heat the oil and cook the pork chops on both sides.
3. Add the remaining ingredients then close the lid.
4. Select the meat/stew function and set the cook time to 30 minutes
5. Release the pressure naturally once the timer beeps.

Lamb Stew

Prep time: 5 minutes

Cook time: 23 minutes

Servings: 2

Nutritional Information:

- Calories: 783
- Fat: 40 g
- Carbs: 32 g
- Protein: 71 g

Ingredients:

- Diced bell peppers, ½ cup
- Fresh thyme
- Pepper, ¼ tsp.
- Oil, 2 tbsp.
- Sliced carrot, 1
- Salt, ¼ tsp.
- Diced onion, 1
- Water, 2 ½ cups
- Minced garlic cloves, 2
- Lamb stewing pieces, ¾ lb.

- Quartered potato, 1

Directions:

1. Press the Sauté function on the instant pot to heat the oil to fry the bell peppers, carrots and onions for 5 minutes.
2. Add garlic and cook for 3 minutes. Remove from fire and set aside.
3. Return liner to Instant Pot then add meat pieces.
4. Add thyme and 2½ cups of water then seal the lid
5. Adjust the cook time to 5 minutes at high pressure
6. Allow natural pressure release for 5 minutes.
7. Unlock lid and add potatoes and sautéed vegetables.
8. Lock lid and select Pressure Cook for 5 minutes. Allow natural pressure release for 10 minutes.
9. Unlock lid when pin in lid drops and serve with toasted bread.

Garlic Pork Tenderloin

Prep time: 5 minutes
Cook time: 8 hours
Servings: 4

Nutritional Information:
- Calories: 252
- Carbs: 1 g
- Protein: 12 g
- Fat: 36 g

Ingredients:
- Pork tenderloin, 3 lbs.
- Thyme, 1 tsp.
- Extra-virgin olive oil, 3 tbsp.
- Minced garlic cloves, 1 head
- Butter, ¼ cup

Directions:
1. Heat the oil and butter in the Instant Pot to fry the thyme and garlic for 4 minutes.
2. Add the pork tenderloin and cook for 3 minutes, stirring.
3. Add 1 cup of water and add the seasonings
4. Switch the vent t venting with the lid closed
5. Select the slow cook button and adjust the time to 8 hours.

Instant Pot Lamb Shanks

Prep time: 15 minutes

Cook time: 40 minutes

Servings: 4

Nutritional Information:

- Calories: 860
- Protein: 43 g
- Carbs: 42 g
- Fats: 22 g

Ingredients:

- Tomato paste, 1 tbsp.
- Chicken stock, 1 cup
- Balsamic vinegar, 2 tbsp.
- Olive oil, 2 tbsp.
- Dried rosemary, 1 tsp.
- Lamb shanks, 4 lbs.
- Unsalted butter, 1½ tbsp.
- Garlic cloves, 8
- Beef stock, ½ cup
- Chopped tomatoes, 4

- Black pepper, 1 tsp.
- Diced red onion, 1
- Ruby Port wine, 1½ cups
- Dried thyme, 1 tsp.
- Dried parsley, 3 tsp.
- Sea salt

Directions:

1. Put oil in the instant pot and select sauté function.
2. Add the lamb shanks to cook until browned on both sides then set aside.
3. Select the sauté function again then put the onion and garlic in the instant pot to cook until soft
4. Add the stock, port wine, lamb juice in the bowl, salt, pepper, chopped tomatoes, herbs, tomato paste, and the lamb shanks.
5. Select the manual function and cook for 30 minutes while covered.
6. Natural release the pressure when the time has elapsed. Transfer the lamb shanks to dish and cover.
7. Add the butter to the Instant Pot and select Sauté.
8. Whisk thoroughly and then add the vinegar in and stir. Pour this sauce in the dish with the lamb shanks.

Lamb Rogan Josh

Prep time: 10 minutes
Cook time: 25 minutes
Servings: 2

Nutritional Information:
- Calories: 383
- Fat: 29 g
- Carbs: 11 g
- Protein: 21 g.

Ingredients:
- Cardamom pods, 3
- Bay leaves, 2

- Cumin seeds, ½ tbsp.
- Whole cloves, 2
- Leg of lamb, 1½ lbs.
- Masala, ½ tbsp.
- Salt, ¼ tsp.
- Olive oil, 1 tbsp.
- Greek yogurt, 4 tbsp.
- Pepper, ¼ tsp.
- Cinnamon bark, 2-inch

Directions:

1. In a mixing bowl, mix the lamb with Garam masala and yogurt.
2. Select sauté function on the instant pot and pour the oil.
3. Add the spice items, except for the powder ingredients and sauté for 3 minutes.
4. Add the garlic, remaining powder ingredients, tomato and a cup of water and cook for 5 minutes.
5. Add the marinated lamb and stir evenly. Close the lid and manually set the time to 10 minutes.
6. Remove the lid and set back to sauté.
7. Stir and cook for about 7 minutes.
8. Serve with cooked rice

Marinara Beef Meatballs

Prep time: 15 minutes
Cook time: 20 minutes
Servings: 4

Nutritional Information:
- Calories: 317
- Protein: 38 g
- Carbs: 32 g
- Fats: 14 g

Ingredients:
- Grated parmesan, 2 tbsp.
- Chopped fresh parsley, 1 bunch
- Black pepper, 1/3 tsp.
- Chopped red onion, ½
- Dried basil, ½ tsp.
- Dried thyme, ½ tsp.
- Minced garlic cloves, 2
- Beaten eggs, 2
- Chicken stock, 1/3 cup
- Salt, ½ tsp.
- Red wine, 3 tbsp.

- Lean ground beef, 1 lb.
- Olive oil, 3 tbsp.
- Red chili pepper flakes, ½ tsp.
- Marinara sauce, 2 ½ cups

Directions:

1. Put the parmesan, parsley, Black pepper, red onion, dried basil, dried thyme, garlic cloves, eggs, salt, beef, and red chili pepper flakes in a bowl
2. Mix thoroughly with the hands.
3. Shape the ground beef mixture into medium balls and refrigerate them for 15 minutes.
4. Select sauté function on the instant pot then add 2 tablespoons of oil.
5. Fry the meatballs in batches until browned evenly.
6. Mix together the stock, Marinara sauce, parsley, and wine then pour 1/3 cup of the mixture into the pot.
7. Add the meatballs and pour over the remaining sauce.
8. Press the manual function and set the cook time to 6 minutes
9. When cooked, allow the pressure to release naturally for 5 minutes before releasing the remaining pressure.

Mushroom Beef Stroganoff

Prep time: 20 minutes
Cook time: 23 minutes
Servings: 2

Nutritional Information:

- Calories: 317
- Carbs: 4 g
- Protein: 36 g
- Fat: 17 g

Ingredients:

- Water, 1 cup
- Salt, 1 ½ tsp.
- Beef stew meat, 1½ lbs.
- Garlic, 1 ½ tbsp.
- Black pepper, 1 ½ tsp.
- Chopped mushroom, 2 cups.
- Sour cream, ¾ cup
- Oil, 1 ½ tbsp.
- Diced onions, ¾ cup

Directions:

1. Press the Sauté button on the instant pot then heat the oil.
2. Add the onions and garlic and cook for 3 minutes,
3. Add the rest of ingredients, except the sour cream.
4. Secure the lid and set the cooker on Manual for 20 minutes at high pressure,
5. When it beeps; Natural Release the steam and remove the lid after 20 minutes.
6. Stir in the sour cream and serve.

Instant Pot Lamb Chops

Prep time: 15 minutes
Cook time: 30 minutes
Servings: 2

Nutritional Information:
- Calories: 579
- Carbs: 14 g
- Protein: 70 g
- Fat: 26 g

Ingredients:
- Sliced carrots, 1 cup
- Arrowroot starch, 1 tbsp.
- Diced tomatoes, ¾ cup
- Black pepper.

- Lamb chops, 1 lb.
- Bone broth, ½ cup
- Butter, 1 ½ tbsp.
- Sliced small onion, ½
- Crushed garlic clove, 1
- Cold water, ½ tbsp.
- Crushed dried rosemary, ¾ tsp.
- Salt

Directions:

1. Press the sauté button on the instant pot then put the butter to melt
2. Add the lamb chops and cook for 3 minutes each side then set aside on a plate
3. Put the garlic and onion into the pot and cook for 4 minutes
4. Top with the remaining ingredients then close the lid
5. Press the manual button then set the cook time to 15 minutes at high pressure
6. Release the steam quickly and remove the lid.
7. In the meantime, mix the arrowroot flour and some water.
8. Pour the mixture into the pot.
9. Cook for 5 minutes then pour this sauce over the fried chops, Serve hot.

Pork Sausages and Mushrooms

Prep time: 10 minutes
Cook time: 35 minutes

Servings: 2

Nutritional Information:

- Calories: 624
- Carbs: 27 g
- Protein: 35 g
- Fat: 42 g

Ingredients:

- Large Portobello mushrooms, 2
- Chopped parsley, ¼ cup
- Marinara sauce, ½ cup
- Ricotta cheese, ½ cup
- Pork sausages, ½ lb.
- Shredded mozzarella cheese, ½ cup

Directions:

1. Stuff each mushroom with pork sausage

2. Place the ricotta cheese over the sausages and carve a dent in the center.
3. Drizzle the marinara sauce over the ricotta cheese
4. Cover with mozzarella cheese on top and place the mushrooms in the instant pot.
5. Secure the lid; select the Manual function and cook for 35 minutes at high pressure
6. Natural release the steam then remove the lid. Serve immediately.

Poultry

Lemongrass and Coconut Chicken

Prep time: 5 minutes
Cook time: 20 minutes
Servings: 2

Nutritional Information:
- Calories: 711
- Carbs: 10 g
- Protein: 62 g
- Fat: 46 g

Ingredients:

- Fish sauce, 2 tbsp.
- Chopped cilantro, ¼ cup
- Chicken drumsticks, 4
- Pepper.
- Sliced lemongrass stalk, 1
- Five spice powder, 1 tsp.
- Sliced onion, 1
- Minced garlic cloves, 4
- Soy sauce, 3 tbsp.
- Ginger piece, 1

- Coconut milk, 1 cup
- Salt

Directions:

1. Press the Sauté function on the Instant Pot then add the chicken, onion, and garlic.
2. Cook until the chicken has slightly browned, for 5 minutes.
3. Add the remaining ingredients.
4. Select the poultry function with the lid closed
5. Set the cooking time to 15 minutes.
6. Release the pressure naturally when the timer clicks

Honey Sesame Chicken

Prep time: 5 minutes
Cook time: 26 minutes
Servings: 4

Nutritional Information:

- Calories: 628
- Carbs: 35 g
- Protein: 64 g
- Fat: 25 g

Ingredients:

- Toasted sesame seeds, 1 tbsp.
- Salt
- Diced onions, ½ cup
- Red pepper flakes, ¼ tsp.
- Skinless chicken breasts, 4
- Sesame oil, 2 tsp.
- Honey, ½ cup
- Pepper.

- Chopped green onion, 2
- Soy sauce, ½ cup
- Ketchup, ¼ cup
- Minced garlic cloves, 2
- Oil, 1 tbsp.

Directions:

1. Select the Sauté button on the Instant Pot.
2. Pour the oil and sauté the onions and garlic until fragrant.
3. Add the chicken meat and season with salt and pepper.
4. Cook for 3 minutes on each side.
5. Add the soy sauce, ketchup, sesame oil, honey, and red pepper flakes.
6. Select the poultry function with the lid closed.
7. Adjust the cooking time to 20 minutes.
8. Release the pressure naturally when the timer clicks.
9. Garnish with onions and sesame seeds.

Instant Pot Cashew Chicken

Prep time: 3 minutes
Cook time: 15 minutes
Servings: 4

Nutritional Information:

- Calories: 444
- Carbs: 11 g
- Protein: 28 g
- Fat: 32 g

Ingredients:

- Rice vinegar, 2 tbsp.
- Chopped green onions, ¼ cup
- Toasted cashew nuts, 1/3 cup
- Water, 2 tbsp.
- Cornstarch, 1 tbsp.
- Skinless chicken thighs, 4.
- Black pepper, ¼ tsp.
- Brown sugar, 1 tbsp.
- Minced garlic clove, 1
- Grated ginger, 1 tsp.
- Ketchup, 2 tbsp.

- Toasted sesame seeds, 2 tbsp.
- Soy sauce, ¼ cup

Directions:

1. Put all ingredients except the cornstarch slurry, cashew nuts, green onions, and sesame seeds in the Instant Pot then stir well.
2. Select the manual function and set the cook time to 15 minutes with the lid closed
3. Release the pressure naturally once the timer clicks.
4. Remove the lid and select sauté button then add the slurry and stir well
5. Allow simmering until the sauce thickens.
6. Add the cashew nuts, green onions, and sesame seeds then serve.

Instant Pot Shredded Chicken

Prep time: 3 minutes
Cook time: 30 minutes
Servings: 5

Nutritional Information:
- Calories: 392
- Carbs: 1 g
- Protein: 47 g
- Fat: 21 g

Ingredients:
- Pepper.
- Water, ½ cup
- Salt
- Chicken breasts, 4 lbs.

Directions:
1. Put all ingredients in the Instant Pot.
2. Select the poultry button with the lid closed then set the cook time to 30 minutes
3. Release the pressure naturally once the timer clicks
4. Shred the chicken meat using 2 forks.

Instant Pot Chicken Cacciatore

/**Prep time:** 5 minutes

Cook time: 20 minutes

Servings: 4

Nutritional Information:

- Calories: 133
- Carbs: 11 g
- Protein: 14 g
- Fat: 3 g

Ingredients:
- Diced red bell pepper, ¼ cup
- Dried oregano, ½ tsp.
- Skinless chicken thighs, 4
- Crushed tomatoes, ½ can
- Salt
- Diced onion, ½ cup
- Bay leaf, 1
- Pepper.
- Diced green bell pepper, ½ cup

Directions:

1. In the Instant Pot, put all the ingredients and stir well.
2. Select the poultry function with the lid closed then set the cook time to 20 minutes.
3. Release the pressure naturally once the timer clicks.

Honey Teriyaki Chicken

Prep time: 3 minutes
Cook time: 15 minutes
Servings: 6

Nutritional Information:

- Calories: 200
- Carbs: 9 g
- Protein: 22 g
- Fat: 9 g

Ingredients:

- Minced garlic cloves, 2
- Rice vinegar, ¼ cup

- Toasted sesame seeds, 2 tbsp.
- Cornstarch, 1 tbsp.
- Chicken thighs, 8
- Soy sauce, ½ cup
- Grated ginger, 2 tsp.
- Black pepper, ¼ tsp.
- Honey, 2 tbsp.
- Water, 2 tbsp.
- Chopped green onions, 2 tbsp.

Directions:

1. Put all ingredients except the cornstarch slurry, sesame seeds, and green onions in the Instant Pot and stir well.
2. Select the manual function and set the cook time to 15 minutes with the lid closed.
3. Release the pressure naturally once the timer clicks.
4. Open the lid and press the Sauté button then add the slurry and stir.
5. Allow simmering until the sauce thickens then sprinkle with sesame seeds and green onions on top.

Instant Pot BBQ Chicken with Potatoes

Prep time: 5 minutes
Cook time: 15 minutes
Servings: 4

Nutritional Information:

- Calories: 254
- Carbs: 29 g
- Protein: 27 g
- Fat: 3 g

Ingredients:
- Water, ½ cup
- Sliced large onion, 1
- BBQ sauce, 1 cup
- Minced garlic, 1 tbsp.
- Peeled and chopped large potatoes, 3
- Italian seasoning, 1 tbsp.
- Chicken breast, 4.

Directions:
1. Into the Instant Pot, put all the ingredients and stir well.
2. Select the poultry function with the lid closed then set the cook time to 15 minutes
3. Release the pressure naturally once the timer clicks.

Chicken with White Wine Mushroom Sauce

Prep time: 5 minutes
Cook time: 20 minutes
Servings: 6

Nutritional Information:
- Calories: 487
- Carbs: 38 g
- Protein: 42 g
- Fat: 21 g

Ingredients:
- Chicken broth, 1 cup
- Pepper.

- Vegetable oil, 2 tbsp.
- Bay leaves, 2
- Chopped onion, 1
- Minced garlic cloves, 4
- Dry white wine, 1 ½ cups
- Thyme, 1 tbsp.
- Salt
- Sliced cremini mushrooms, 1¼ lbs.
- Cornstarch, 2 tbsp.
- Halved chicken breasts, 6
- Water, 2 tbsp.
- Lemon juice, 1 tbsp.

Directions:

1. Press the Sauté button on the Instant Pot then add the oil to heat.
2. Add the chicken, onion and garlic
3. Cook as you stir until the chicken meat has turned lightly golden.
4. Add the broth, bay leaves, dry white wine, mushrooms, thyme, lemon juice, and seasonings.
5. Select the poultry function with the lid closed then set the cook time to 15 minutes.
6. Release the pressure naturally once the timer clicks.
7. Remove the lid and select the Sauté button then add the cornstarch slurry as you stir.
8. Allow simmering until the sauce thickens.

Root Beer Chicken Wings

Prep time: 5 minutes
Cook time: 10 minutes
Servings: 4

Nutritional Information:
- Calories: 229
- Carbs: 18 g
- Protein: 26 g
- Fat: 6 g

Ingredients:
- Root beer, 2 cans
- Soy sauce, ¼ cup
- Chicken wings, 2 lbs.
- Sugar, ¼ cup

Directions:
1. Into the Instant Pot, put all the ingredients and stir well.
2. Select the poultry function with the lid closed then set the cook time to 10 minutes
3. Release the pressure naturally once the timer clicks.

Sticky Chicken and Chilies

Prep time: 5 minutes

Cook time: 15 minutes

Servings: 6

Nutritional Information:

- Calories: 522
- Carbs: 12 g
- Protein: 36 g
- Fat: 37 g

Ingredients:

- Currants, 2 tbsp.
- Chicken thighs, 8
- Chili paste, 1 ½ tbsp.
- Chicken broth, ½ cup
- Balsamic vinegar, 2 tbsp.
- Rind, 1 small lemon
- Honey, ¼ cup
- Olive oil, 2 tbsp.
- Minced garlic cloves, 2

Directions:

1. Put all ingredients in the Instant Pot except for the cornstarch slurry.
2. Press the poultry button with the lid closed
3. Adjust the cooking time to 15 minutes.
4. Release the pressure naturally once the timer clicks.

Balsamic Orange Chicken Drumsticks

Prep time: 5 minutes

Cook time: 15 minutes

Servings: 4

Nutritional Information:
- Calories: 281
- Carbs: 15 g
- Protein: 26 g
- Fat: 14 g

Ingredients:
- Orange marmalade, 1/3 cup

- Chicken drumsticks, 8
- Honey, 2 tbsp.
- Balsamic vinegar, 2 tbsp.
- Freshly squeezed orange juice, 1/3 cup
- Olive oil, 1 tbsp.

Directions:
1. Press the Sauté button on the Instant Pot.
2. Heat the oil and place the chicken drumsticks. Stir to brown all edges.
3. Pour in the rest of the ingredients.
4. Select the poultry function with the lid closed.
5. Adjust the cooking time to 15 minutes.
6. Release the pressure naturally once the timer clicks.

Ginger Turkey and Potatoes

Prep time: 6 minutes
Cook time: 25 minutes
Servings: 2

Nutritional Information:

- Calories: 614
- Carbs: 86 g
- Protein: 28 g
- Fat: 11 g

Ingredients:

- Cubed potatoes, 2
- Chopped cilantro, 1 tbsp.
- Grated ginger, 1 tbsp.
- Sweet paprika, 1 tbsp.
- Skinless sliced turkey breast, 1
- Chopped green onions, 2
- Black pepper
- Avocado oil, 1 tbsp.
- Minced garlic cloves, 2
- Salt
- Chicken stock, 1½ cups

Directions:

1. Set your instant pot on Sauté mode, add the oil, heat it, and add the ginger, paprika, garlic and the meat and brown for 5 minutes.
2. Add the remaining ingredients, put the lid on, and cook on High for 20 minutes.
3. Release the pressure naturally for 10 minutes, divide everything between plates and serve.

Turkey and Pomegranate Mix

Prep time: 10 minutes

Cook time: 30 minutes

Servings: 2

Nutritional Information:
- Calories: 263
- Fat: 8 g
- Carbs: 7 g
- Protein: 12 g

Ingredients:
- Chopped cilantro, 1 tbsp.
- Black pepper, ¼ tsp.
- Pomegranate seeds, 1 cup

- Sweet paprika, 1 tbsp.
- Sliced turkey breast, 1
- Chicken stock, 1 cup
- Salt, ¼ tsp.
- Olive oil, 1 tbsp.

Directions:

1. Set the instant pot on Sauté mode, add the oil, heat it up, add the meat and cook for 5 minutes.
2. Add the rest of the ingredients, put the lid on and cook on High for 25 minutes.
3. Release the pressure naturally for 10 minutes, divide everything between plates and serve.

Chicken Wings and Scallions Sauce

Prep time: 10 minutes
Cook time: 25 minutes
Servings: 4

Nutritional Information:

- Calories: 224
- Fat: 11 g
- Carbs: 9 g
- Protein: 11 g

Ingredients:

- Tomato sauce, 8 oz.
- Black pepper, ¼ tsp.
- Chopped cilantro, ¼ cup
- 1 tbsp. olive oil
- Chicken wings, 8
- Chopped scallions, 6
- Chicken stock, 2 cups
- Salt, ¼ tsp.
- Garlic powder, ½ tsp.
- Chopped tomato, 1

Directions:

1. Set your instant pot on Sauté mode, add the oil, heat it up, add the scallions, garlic powder, salt and pepper and sauté for 5 minutes.
2. Add the chicken wings and brown for 5 minutes more.
3. Add the remaining ingredients, put the lid on and cook on High for 15 minutes.
4. Release the pressure naturally for 10 minutes, divide everything between plates and serve.

Turkey and Cauliflower Sauté

Prep time: 10 minutes
Cook time: 35 minutes
Servings: 3

Nutritional Information:
- Calories: 262
- Fat: 12 g
- Carbs: 7 g
- Protein: 16 g

Ingredients:
- Olive oil, 2 tbsp.
- Dried rosemary, ¼ tsp.

- Cauliflower florets, 1 cup
- Chopped yellow onion, 1
- Black pepper, ¼ tsp.
- Sliced turkey breast, 2 lbs.
- Salt, ¼ tsp.
- Chicken stock, 1 cup
- Minced garlic cloves, 2

Directions:

1. Set your instant pot on Sauté mode, add the oil, heat it up, add the onion, cauliflower, garlic, rosemary, salt and pepper, toss and sauté for 10 minutes.
2. Add the turkey and the stock, put the lid on and cook on High for 25 minutes.
3. Release the pressure naturally for 10 minutes, divide the mix between plates and serve.

Turkey and Mushrooms Meatballs

Prep time: 10 minutes
Cook time: 30 minutes
Servings: 3

Nutritional Information:

- Calories: 361
- Fat: 9 g
- Carbs: 12 g
- Protein: 8 g

Ingredients:

- Chopped parsley, ¼ cup

- Almond meal, ½ cup
- Minced garlic cloves, 4
- Sliced white mushrooms, 10
- Olive oil, 2 tbsp.
- Black pepper, ¼ tsp.
- Grated parmesan, ¼ cup
- Ground turkey meat, 1 lb.
- Salt, ¼ tsp.
- Whisked egg, 1
- Chopped red onion, 1
- Tomato sauce, 1 ½ cups

Directions:

1. In a bowl, mix the turkey meat with the other ingredients except the sauce and the oil, stir well and shape medium meatballs out of this mix.
2. Set the instant pot on Sauté mode, add the oil, heat it up, add the meatballs and cook them on both sides for 2 minutes each.
3. Add the sauce, put the lid on and cook on High for 25 minutes.
4. Release the pressure naturally for 10 minutes, divide everything between plates and serve.

Lime Turkey Wings

Prep time: 10 minutes
Cook time: 30 minutes
Servings: 4

Nutritional Information:
- Calories: 231
- Fat: 11 g
- Carbs: 7 g
- Protein: 18 g

Ingredients:
- Avocado oil, 1 tbsp.
- Chicken stock, 1 cup
- Chopped yellow onion, 1

- Black pepper, ¼ tsp.
- Halved turkey wings, 6
- Lime juice, 2 tbsp.
- Minced garlic cloves, 4
- Salt, ¼ tsp.
- Grated lime zest, 1 tbsp.

Directions:

1. Set your instant pot on sauté mode, add the oil, heat it up, add the onion and sauté for 2 minutes.
2. Add the turkey and the rest of the ingredients, put the lid on and cook on High for 28 minutes.
3. Release the pressure naturally for 10 minutes, divide everything between plates and serve.

Seafood

Spicy Prawns

Prep time: 5 minutes

Cook time: 5 minutes

Servings: 2

Nutritional Information:

- Calories: 174
- Carbs: 2 g
- Protein: 9 g
- Fat: 15 g

Ingredients:

- Red pepper flakes, 1 tbsp.
- Butter, 1 tbsp.
- Minced garlic cloves, 3
- Pepper
- Olive oil, 3 tbsp.
- Prawns, 1 ½ lb.
- Salt

Directions:

1. Put all ingredients in the Instant Pot.
2. Add ¼ cup of water, salt, and pepper.
3. Switch the vent to sealing with the lid closed.
4. Select the manual function then set the cook time to 5 minutes
5. Release the pressure naturally once the timer clicks.

Thai Fish Curry

Prep time: 5 minutes
Cook time: 10 minutes
Servings: 3

Nutritional Information:
- Calories: 470
- Carbs: 6 g
- Protein: 26 g
- Fat: 10 g

Ingredients:
- Salmon fillets, 1½ lbs.
- Salt
- Curry powder, 2 tbsp.
- Olive oil, 1/3 cup
- Pepper
- Chopped cilantro, ¼ cup
- Freshly squeezed coconut milk, 2 cups

Directions:
1. Into the Instant Pot, put all the ingredients then stir well.
2. Switch the vent to sealing with the lid closed.
3. Select the manual function of the instant pot and set the cook time to 10 minutes
4. Release the pressure naturally once the timer clicks.

Buttered Trout

Prep time: 5 minutes
Cook time: 6 hours
Servings: 2

Nutritional Information:
- Calories: 284
- Carbs: 3 g
- Protein: 7 g
- Fat: 28 g

Ingredients:
- Butter, 3 tbsp.
- Orange zest, 1 tbsp.
- Pepper.
- 1 large trout fillet
- Olive oil, 1 tbsp.
- Salt

Directions:
1. Put all ingredients in the Instant Pot.
2. Switch the vent to venting with the lid closed
3. Press the "Slow Cook" button and adjust the time to 6 hours.
4. Halfway through the cooking time, open the lid and turn over the fish.
5. Continue cooking until the trout forms a hard crust on the surface.

Spicy Chili Garlic Trout

Prep time: 5 minutes
Cook time: 6 hours
Servings: 5

Nutritional Information:

- Calories: 182
- Carbs: 1 g
- Protein: 12 g
- Fat: 16 g

Ingredients:

- Crushed red pepper flakes, 1 tsp.
- Pepper.
- Trout fillets, 2½ lbs.
- Garlic minced cloves, 6
- Salt
- Olive oil, 3 tbsp.

Directions:

1. In the Instant Pot, put all the ingredients and adjust the moisture by adding ¼ cup of water.
2. Switch the vent to venting with the lid sealed
3. Select the slow cook function and cook for 6 hours.

Spicy Lemon Halibut

Prep time: 5 minutes
Cook time: 8 minutes
Servings: 4

Nutritional Information:
- Calories: 770
- Carbs: 4 g
- Protein: 59 g
- Fat: 57 g

Ingredients:
- Chili pepper flakes, 2 tbsp.
- Halibut fillets, 4
- Salt
- Sliced lemons, 2
- Pepper.

Directions:
1. Put the steamer basket in the Instant Pot.
2. Pour a cup of water.
3. Season the halibut fillets with chili pepper flakes, salt, and pepper.
4. Place on the trivet and arrange slices of lemons.
5. Press the manual button with the lid closed then set the cook time to 8 minutes.
6. Do natural pressure release.

Green Chili Mahi Mahi

Prep time: 3 minutes
Cook time: 8 minutes
Servings: 2

Nutritional Information:
- Calories: 368
- Carbs: 11 g
- Protein: 20 g
- Fat: 28 g

Ingredients:
- Enchilada sauce, ¼ cup
- Pepper.

- Butter, 2 tbsp.
- Salt
- Fresh Mahi Mahi fillets, 2

Directions:

1. Put all ingredients except for the butter in the Instant Pot.
2. Press the manual function with the lid closed and set the cook time to 8 minutes.
3. Release the pressure naturally once the timer clicks.
4. Once the lid is open, add the butter.

Wild Alaskan Cod

Prep time: 3 minutes
Cook time: 8 minutes
Servings: 2

Nutritional Information:
- Calories: 135
- Carbs: 1 g
- Protein: 18 g
- Fat: 6 g

Ingredients:
- Pepper.
- Butter, 2 tbsp
- Chopped cherry tomatoes, 1 cup
- Salt
- Wild Alaskan cod fillets, 2

Directions:
1. Put all ingredients except for the butter in the Instant Pot.
2. Select the manual button with the lid closed then set the cook time to 8 minutes.
3. Release the pressure naturally once the timer clicks.
4. Open the lid then add the butter.

Instant Pot Shrimps

Prep time: 1 minute
Cook time: 3 minutes
Servings: 3

Nutritional Information:
- Calories: 150
- Carbs: 2 g
- Protein: 24 g
- Fat: 5 g

Ingredients:
- Butter, 2 tbsp.
- Pepper.
- Parsley, 1 tbsp.
- Shrimp, 2 lbs.
- Minced garlic, 1 tbsp.
- Chicken stock, ½ cup
- Salt
- White wine, ½ cup
- Lemon juice, 1 tbsp.

Directions:
1. Put all ingredients in the Instant Pot.
2. Select the manual function with the lid closed and set the cook time to 3 minutes.
3. Release the pressure naturally once the timer clicks.

Crabs in Coconut Milk

Prep time: 2 minutes
Cook time: 6 minutes
Servings: 2

Nutritional Information:

- Calories: 171
- Carbs: 5 g
- Protein: 15 g
- Fat: 10 g

Ingredients:

- Minced garlic cloves, 3
- Sliced ginger piece, 1
- Pepper.
- Halved crabs, 1 lb.
- Lemongrass stalk, 1
- Chopped onion, 1
- Salt
- Coconut milk, 1 can

Directions:

1. Place all ingredients in the Instant Pot.
2. Press the manual function with the lid closed then set the cook time to 6 minutes.
3. Release the pressure naturally once the timer clicks.

Instant Pot Seafood Stew

Prep time: 5 minutes
Cook time: 10 minutes
Servings: 2

Nutritional Information:
- Calories: 262
- Carbs: 5 g
- Protein: 39 g
- Fat: 9 g

Ingredients:
- Sliced onion, 1
- Bay leaves, 2
- Olive oil, 3 tbsp.

- Fish stock, 1 cup
- Minced garlic cloves, 2
- Cleaned neck clams, 12
- Paprika, 2 tsp.
- Pepper.
- Peeled and deveined shrimps, 1 lb.
- Diced tomatoes, 1 ½ cups
- Salt
- Sliced green bell pepper, 1
- Sliced cod, 1 ½ lbs.

Directions:
1. Press the Sauté button on the Instant Pot.
2. Heat the oil and sauté the onions and garlic until fragrant.
3. Add the fish, shrimps, and clams. Stir for a few minutes.
4. Pour in the rest of the ingredients.
5. Press the manual function with the lid closed then set the cook time to 10 minutes.
6. Release the pressure naturally once the timer clicks.

Lobster with Wine and Tomatoes

Prep time: 5 minutes

Cook time: 10 minutes

Servings: 4

Nutritional Information:

- Calories: 300
- Carbs: 13 g
- Protein: 15 g
- Fat: 15 g

Ingredients:

- Shelled lobsters, 2
- Minced garlic cloves, 2
- Tarragon, 1 tbsp.
- Olive oil, 4 tbsp.
- Diced onions, 2
- Chopped carrot, 1
- Ripe tomatoes, 1 lb.
- Clam juice, 1/3 cup
- Tomato paste, 2 tbsp.
- Cognac, ½ cup

Directions:

1. Press the Sauté button on the Instant Pot.
2. Heat the oil and sauté the onions and garlic until fragrant.
3. Add the rest of the ingredients.
4. Stir to combine.
5. Press the manual function with the lid sealed and set the cook time to 10 minutes.
6. Release the pressure naturally once the timer clicks.

Creamy Haddock with Kale

Prep time: 4 minutes
Cook time: 10 minutes
Servings: 4

Nutritional Information:

- Calories: 327
- Carbs: 6 g
- Protein: 37 g
- Fat: 16 g

Ingredients:

- Chopped kale leaves, 1 cup
- Butter, 2 tbsp.
- Wild Haddock fillets, 4
- Minced garlic cloves, 2
- Pepper.
- Chicken broth, 2 cups
- Chopped onion, 1
- Basil, 1 tbsp.
- Salt
- Crushed red pepper flakes, 1 tsp.
- Heavy cream, ½ cup

Directions:

1. Press the Sauté button on the Instant Pot.
2. Heat the butter and sauté the onion until fragrant.
3. Stir in the rest of the ingredients.
4. Give a good stir.
5. Press the manual function with the lid sealed then set the cook time to 10 minutes.
6. Release the pressure naturally once the timer clicks.

Vegetable mains

Curried Squash Stew

Prep time: 2 minutes
Cook time: 10 minutes
Servings: 4

Nutritional Information:
- Calories: 123
- Carbs: 2 g
- Protein: 9 g
- Fat: 9 g

Ingredients:
- Chopped squash, 2 cups
- Pepper.
- Full-fat coconut milk, 1 can
- Rinsed baby spinach, 1 bag
- Salt
- Garam masala, 2 tbsp.

Directions:
1. Place all ingredients except for the spinach in the Instant Pot.
2. Stir the contents and close the lid.

3. Press the manual setting with the lid closed then set the cook time to 10 minutes.
4. Release the pressure naturally once the timer clicks.
5. Once the lid is open, press the Sauté button.
6. Add the spinach and continue cooking until the greens have wilted.

Instant Pot Zucchini Casserole

Prep time: 2 minutes
Cook time: 6 minutes
Servings: 4

Nutritional Information:

- Calories: 256
- Carbs: 14 g
- Protein: 6 g
- Fat: 2 g

Ingredients:

- Chopped celery stalks, 4
- Sliced zucchinis, 2

- Salt
- Favorite seasoning, 1 package
- Beaten eggs, 4
- Chopped large onions, 1
- Pepper.
- Vegetable stock, ½ cup

Directions:

1. Place all ingredients in the Instant Pot.
2. Stir the contents and close the lid.
3. Press the manual setting then set the cook time to 6 minutes.
4. Do natural pressure release.

Creamy Artichoke, Garlic, and Zucchini

Prep time: 2 minutes

Cook time: 10 minutes

Servings: 6

Nutritional Information:
- Calories: 33
- Carbs: 2 g
- Protein: 1g
- Fat: 3 g

Ingredients:
- Pepper.

- Vegetable broth, ½ cup
- Coconut oil, 2 tbsp.
- Sliced artichoke hearts, 1
- Salt
- Minced garlic, 1
- Sliced medium zucchinis, 2
- Whipping cream, ½ cup

Directions:

1. Press the Sauté button and heat the oil
2. Sauté the garlic until fragrant.
3. Add the rest of the ingredients.
4. Stir the contents and close the lid.
5. Press the manual function and set the cook time to 10 minutes
6. Release the pressure naturally once the timer clicks.

Rosemary Garlic Potatoes

Prep time: 10 minutes
Cook time: 30 minutes
Servings: 2

Nutritional Information:

- Calories: 119
- Carbs: 20 g
- Protein: 2 g
- Fat: 3 g

Ingredients:

- Garlic cloves, 2
- Salt, ½ tsp.

- Rosemary sprigs, 2
- Olive oil, 1 tbsp.
- Sliced potatoes, 1 lb.

Directions:

1. Put the steamer basket in the Instant Pot and pour in 1 cup of water.
2. Take a baking tray that fit in the instant pot and put all the ingredients, mix to coat evenly then cover with aluminum foil.
3. Put the baking dish on the steamer basket
4. Press the steam function with the lid closed then adjust the cook time to 30 minutes.
5. Release the pressure naturally once the timer clicks.

Sweet Sticky Carrots

Prep time: 10 minutes
Cook time: 8 minutes
Servings: 4

Nutritional Information:

- Calories: 63
- Carbs: 12 g
- Protein: 1 g
- Fat: 2 g

Ingredients:
- Raisins, ¼ cup
- Maple syrup, 1 tbsp.
- Pepper
- Melted butter, 1 tbsp.
- Peeled carrots, 2 lbs.

Directions:
1. Put the carrots and raisins in the Instant Pot.
2. Add a cup of water and close the lid.
3. Select the Steam button and set the cook time to 6 minutes.

4. Do natural pressure release to open the lid.
5. Drain the carrots and raisins to remove excess water.
6. Meanwhile, press the Sauté button on the Instant Pot and heat the butter.
7. Add the maple syrup and add the carrots and raisins back to the pressure cooker. Add pepper to taste.
8. Allow simmering for 2 minutes.

Instant Pot Steamed Artichoke

Prep time: 5 minutes

Cook time: 5 minutes

Servings: 6

Nutritional Information:
- Calories: 548
- Carbs: 14 g
- Protein: 4 g
- Fat: 46 g

Ingredients:
- Olive oil, 2 cups
- Water, 2 cups
- Juiced lemons, 2
- Minced garlic cloves, 3
- Peppercorns, 1 tbsp.
- Trimmed artichokes, 6

Directions:
1. Pour the water and juice from one lemon in the pressure cooker.
2. Place the artichokes, peppercorns, garlic and olive oil in the pressure cooker
3. Press the manual function with the lid closed and set the cook time to 5 minutes.
4. Release the pressure naturally once the timer clicks.

Simple Green Beans Salad

Prep time: 5 minutes
Cook time: 6 minutes
Servings: 6

Nutritional Information:
- Calories: 181
- Carbs: 33 g
- Protein: 8 g
- Fat: 3 g

Ingredients:
- Sliced potatoes, 2 lbs.
- Balsamic vinegar, 1 tbsp.

- Pepper.
- Porcini mushrooms, 1 oz.
- Salt
- Boiling water, 1 cup
- Olive oil, 1 tbsp.
- Trimmed green beans, 2 lbs.

Directions:

1. Place the mushrooms, potatoes, and beans in the Instant Pot.
2. Pour enough water to boil.
3. Press the manual function with the lid closed and set the cook time to 6 minutes
4. Release the pressure naturally once the timer clicks.
5. Take the vegetables out and drain the water.
6. Place the veggies to cool in a salad bowl
7. Add balsamic vinegar, salt, olive oil, and pepper then toss to coat.

Simple Eggplant Spread

Prep time: 5 minutes
Cook time: 10 minutes
Servings: 6

Nutritional Information:
- Calories: 155
- Carbs: 17 g
- Protein: 2 g
- Fat: 12 g

Ingredients:
- Tahini, 1 tbsp.
- Juiced lemon, 1
- Olive oil, 4 tbsp.

- Extra virgin oil
- Salt, 1 tsp.
- Water, 1 cup
- Sliced eggplant, 2 lbs.
- Thyme
- Sliced black olives, ¼ cup
- Garlic cloves, 4

Directions:

1. Press the Sauté button on the pressure cooker.
2. Heat the oil and add the sliced eggplants. Fry the eggplants for 4 minutes on each side.
3. Add the garlic and sauté until fragrant. Season with salt.
4. Add a cup of water and close the lid.
5. Press the Manual button and adjust the cooking time to 6 minutes.
6. Do natural pressure release and take the eggplants out and transfer to a food processor.
7. Add salt, lemon juice, and tahini.
8. Pulse until smooth.
9. Place in a bowl and garnish with olives, thyme and a dash of extra virgin olive oil.

Instant Pot Mashed Potatoes

Prep time: 5 minutes
Cook time: 30 minutes
Servings: 4

Nutritional Information:

- Calories: 153
- Carbs: 21 g
- Protein: 3 g
- Fat: 7 g

Ingredients:

- Water, 1 cup
- Pepper.
- Milk, 2/3 cup
- Butter, 4 tbsp.
- Salt
- Quartered potatoes, 2 lbs.

Directions:

1. Put the steamer basket in the Instant Pot and pour 1 cup of water.
2. Put the potatoes on top of the steamer.

3. Press the steam button with the lid closed and set the cook time to 30 minutes.
4. Release the pressure naturally when the timer clicks.
5. Put the cooked potatoes on a bowl and mash together with the other ingredients.
6. Serve warm.

Desserts

Sweet Apple Pudding

Prep time: 5 minutes

Cook time: 10 minutes

Servings: 6

Nutritional Information:
- Calories: 271
- Carbs: 62 g
- Protein: 3 g
- Fat: 3 g

Ingredients:
- Raw honey, ½ cup

- Cinnamon, 2 tsp.
- Coconut sugar, ½ cup
- Sea salt, 1 tsp.
- Allspice, ¼ tsp.
- Milk, 2 cups
- Lemon juice, 2 tbsp.
- Vanilla, 2 tsp.
- Chopped apples, 6
- Ground nutmeg, ¼ tsp.

Directions:

1. Into the Instant Pot, put all the ingredients and stir well.
2. Press the manual function with the lid closed
3. Adjust the cooking time to 10 minutes.
4. Release the pressure naturally when the timer clicks

Pumpkin and Rice Pudding

Prep time: 10 minutes
Cook time: 25 minutes

Servings: 3

Nutritional Information:

- Calories: 412
- Carbs: 62 g
- Protein: 12 g
- Fat: 14 g

Ingredients:

- Pumpkin puree, 1 cup
- Chopped pitted dates, ½ cup
- Cinnamon stick, 1
- Short grain rice, 1 cup
- Water, ½ cup
- Maple syrup, ½ cup
- Salt, 1/8 tsp.
- Pumpkin spice mix, 1 tsp.
- Vanilla extract, 1 tsp.
- Milk, 3 cups

Directions:

1. Soak rice with water and let it rest for at least 10 minutes.
2. Without the lid on, press the Sauté button on the Instant Pot and add milk and water. Add the rice. Bring to a boil and add rice, dates, and cinnamon. Season with salt.
3. Lock the lid and press the Rice button.
4. Adjust the cooking time to 20 minutes.
5. Do natural pressure release to open the lid.
6. Once the lid is open, press the Sauté button and add the pumpkin puree, spice mix, maple syrup and vanilla extract.
7. Allow simmering for 5 minutes
8. Remove the cinnamon stick before serving.

Steamed Carrot Cake

Prep time: 20 minutes
Cook time: 50 minutes

Servings: 8

Nutritional Information:
- Calories: 428
- Carbs: 32 g
- Protein: 4 g
- Fat: 32 g

Ingredients:
- Nutmeg, ½ tsp.
- Molasses, ¼ cup
- Butter, 4 tbsp.
- Frozen and grated shortening, 2/3 cup
- Flour, ½ cup
- Cinnamon, ½ tsp.
- Ground cinnamon, ¼ tsp.
- Allspice, ½ tsp.
- Chopped pecans, ½ cup
- Salt, ¼ tsp.
- Brown sugar, 1 cup
- Baking soda, ½ tsp.
- Rum, 2 tbsp.

- Raisins, ½ cup
- Eggs, 2
- Breadcrumbs, 1 cup
- Cream, ¼ cup
- Grated carrots, ½ cup

Directions:

1. Put the steamer basket in the Instant Pot and add 1 cup of water.
2. In a mixing bowl, whisk ½ cup of brown sugar, molasses, and eggs.
3. Pour in the flour and the spices, baking soda, salt, shortening, carrots, bread crumbs, and pecans.
4. Transfer the batter into a baking dish that will fit the pressure cooker. Cover with aluminum foil and place on the steamer.
5. Press the steam button with the lid closed and set the cook time to 50 minutes
6. Prepare the rum sauce by mixing in a saucepan the remaining brown sugar, butter, cream, rum, and cinnamon. Heat over low flame until reduced.
7. Once the pressure cooker beeps, do natural pressure release.
8. Pour over the rum sauce on top.
9. Allow to cool before serving.

Instant Pot Cherry Compote

Prep time: 5 minutes

Cook time: 15 minutes

Servings: 8

Nutritional Information:
- Calories: 46
- Carbs: 12 g
- Protein: 1 g
- Fat: 1 g

Ingredients:
- Almond extract, ¼ tsp.
- Frozen cherries, 1 package

- Sugar, ¾ cup
- Water, 2 tbsp.
- Cornstarch, 2 tbsp.
- Lemon juice, 2 tbsp.

Directions:

1. Put the sugar, lemon juice cherries in the Instant Pot and stir.
2. Press the manual function with the lid closed then set the cook time to 10 minutes.
3. Do natural pressure release.
4. Meanwhile, mix the cornstarch, water and almond extract.
5. Once the lid is open, press the Sauté button and pour the slurry over the cherries.
6. Gently stir the mixture and allow to simmer until the sauce thickens

Instant Pot Raspberry Curd

Prep time: 5 minutes
Cook time: 5 minutes
Servings: 6

Nutritional Information:

- Calories: 148
- Carbs: 24 g
- Protein: 2 g
- Fat: 6 g

Ingredients:

- Butter, 2 tbsp.
- Raspberries, 12 oz.

- Sugar, 1 cup
- Egg yolks, 2
- Lemon juice, 2 tbsp.

Directions:

1. Put the lemon juice, sugar, and raspberries in the Instant Pot.
2. Press the manual setting with the lid closed then adjust the cook time to 5 minutes.
3. Release the pressure naturally when the timer clicks and remove the lid.
4. Strain the raspberries to puree and remove large lumps and seeds. Discard the seeds.
5. Beat the egg yolks in another bowl and add the raspberry puree. Return to the Instant Pot.
6. Without the lid on, press the Sauté button and stir constantly.
7. Add the butter and wait for the mixture to thicken.

Apple Cinnamon Cake

Prep time: 10 minutes
Cook time: 30 minutes

Servings: 6

Nutritional Information:

- Calories: 204
- Carbs: 29 g
- Protein: 1 g
- Fat: 10 g

Ingredients:

- Melted coconut oil, ¼ cup
- Almond flour, 2 cups
- Grated fresh nutmeg, 1 tsp.
- Cinnamon, 1 tsp.
- Vanilla, 1 tbsp.
- Salt, ½ tsp.
- Raw honey, ½ cup
- Arrowroot powder, ¼ cup
- Diced apple, 1
- Baking soda, ½ tsp.
- Large egg, 1

Directions:
1. Put the steamer basket in the Instant Pot.
2. In a mixing bowl, combine all ingredients.
3. Pour into a baking dish that will fit in the Instant Pot then cover with an aluminum foil.
4. Place on top of the steamer basket.
5. Press the steam button with the lid closed and set the cook time to 30 minutes.
6. Do natural pressure release.

Cranberry Stuffed Apples

Prep time: 10 minutes
Cook time: 30 minutes
Servings: 5

Nutritional Information:

- Calories: 136
- Carbs: 31 g
- Protein: 1 g
- Fat: 2 g

Ingredients:

- Chopped walnuts, 2 tbsp.
- Ground nutmeg, 1/8 tsp.
- Chopped fresh cranberries, 1/3 cup
- Ground cinnamon, ¼ tsp.
- Packed brown sugar, ¼ cup
- Cored medium apples, 5

Directions:

1. Put the steamer basket in the Instant Pot and pour 1 cup of water

2. Place the cored apples in a baking dish that will fit in the Instant Pot.
3. In a mixing bowl, combine the cranberries, walnuts, sugar, cinnamon, and nutmeg.
4. Spoon the mixture into the hollowed center of the apples then cover with an aluminum foil.
5. Place on the steamer rack and then select the steam function with the lid closed
6. Adjust the cooking time to 30 minutes.
7. Do natural pressure release.

Conclusion

Thank you again for purchasing this book!

I hope that the contents of this cookbook were insightful and able to provide you with the knowledge to get the most from your instant pot, as well as plenty of recipes to try out and enjoy! If you want to take healthier or if you are looking to save more time during the day, the instant pot has the ability to assist you!

The next step is to pick out some recipes that caught your eye and give them a go! What do you have to lose? And if you have yet to purchase yourself an instant pot, what is stopping you? A one-time purchase means spending hundreds of dollars less on convenient fast-food meals and literally have the capability of creating time from thin air! It's safe to say that an instant pot is totally worth the investment.

Finally, if you enjoyed this book, then I'd like to ask you for a favor, would you be kind enough to leave a review for this book on Amazon? It'd be greatly appreciated!

Julie

Text Copyright © Julie Bower

All rights reserved. No part of this guide may be reproduced in any form without permission in writing from the publisher except in the case of brief quotations embodied in critical articles or reviews.

Legal & Disclaimer

The information contained in this book and its contents is not designed to replace or take the place of any form of medical or professional advice; and is not meant to replace the need for independent medical, financial, legal or other professional advice or services, as may be required. The content and information in this book has been provided for educational and entertainment purposes only.

The content and information contained in this book has been compiled from sources deemed reliable, and it is accurate to the best of the Author's knowledge, information and belief. However, the Author cannot guarantee its accuracy and validity and cannot be held liable for any errors and/or omissions. Further, changes are periodically made to this book as and when needed. Where appropriate and/or necessary, you must consult a professional (including but not limited to your doctor, attorney, financial advisor or such other professional advisor) before using any of the suggested remedies, techniques, or information in this book.

Upon using the contents and information contained in this book, you agree to hold harmless the Author from and against any damages, costs, and expenses, including any legal fees potentially resulting from the application of any of the information provided by this book. This disclaimer applies to any loss, damages or injury caused by the use and application, whether directly or indirectly, of any advice or information presented, whether for breach of contract, tort, negligence, personal injury, criminal intent, or under any other cause of action.

You agree to accept all risks of using the information presented inside this book.

You agree that by continuing to read this book, where appropriate and/or necessary, you shall consult a professional (including but not limited to your doctor, attorney, or financial advisor or such other advisor as needed) before using any of the suggested remedies, techniques, or information in this book.

www.ingramcontent.com/pod-product-compliance
Lightning Source LLC
Chambersburg PA
CBHW072158100526
44589CB00015B/2271